C000184956

Teashop
in KENT

The Quay at Sandwich was once a thriving and bustling port, one of the busiest in England. Today the route to the sea has silted up and the port is open only to small craft.

Rupert Matthews

S.B. Publications

First published in 2010 by S. B. Publications
Tel: 01323 893498
Email: sbpublications@tiscali.co.uk
www.sbpublications.co.uk

ISBN 978-1-85770-355-9

Designed and Typeset by EH Graphics (01273) 515527

Front cover photo: Lympne Castle from the lane near Selby Farm, Burmarsh.
Back cover photo: Boy Court Lane, Headcorn.

Contents

Teashop Walks in Kent

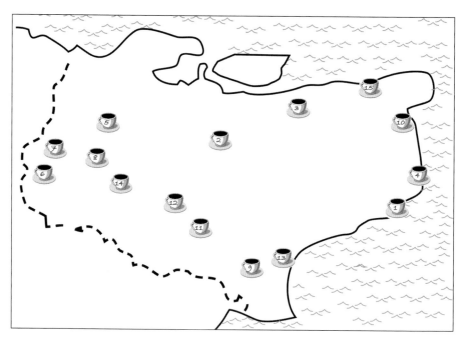

Short Walks
1 Dover
2 Lenham
3 Hernhill

Medium Walks
4 Walmer
5 West Malling
6 Penshurst
7 Otford
8 Hadlow
9 Appledore
10 Sandwich

Longer Walks
11 Tenterden
12 Headcorn
13 Burmarsh
14 Goudhurst
15 Birchington

Map Key

🏰 Castle / Tower	∿∿	Sea
Church with tower	⌒	River, canal or waterway
• Church with steeple	⋯	Unsurfaced footpath
● Station		Surfaced path or track
🕈 Windmill		
■ Other building		Lane
Deciduous woodland		Road
Coniferous woodland		
Mixed woodland		Main road
Teashop		
Pub	①	Instruction point

Introduction

"Afternoon tea is the finest contribution that England has made to cuisine", or so my grandmother always had it. And she was in a position to know. My childhood memories are filled with images of that kindly lady cutting Victoria sponges, handing round buttered scones and pouring out cups (never mugs) of nice fresh tea.

Ever since those long off days I have had a particular affinity for afternoon tea. I like to keep a cake on the go at home so that, come 4 o'clock, I can cut off a slice and take a break from the work of writing to sip a hot cup of tea and munch on the cake. I'm sure my wife thinks I'm a bit odd.

Essential as a cuppa and a cake at the desk might be to the working day, it cannot possibly compare with a visit to a traditional tea shop. I might have a cake at home, but a good tea-shop will have a whole range of cakes from which slices can be carved as well as a range of buns, pastries and scones. And if you are lucky there will be cucumber sandwiches on offer as well. There is nothing quite like a good teashop. I confess that I am totally unable to see one without wanting to pop in.

Addicted as I might be to the delights of a cream tea, I know full well that the tasty dainties can add worryingly to the waistline. So all visits to a teashop should be accompanied by a bit of light exercise - a walk.

Such is the purpose of this book.

I have selected 15 of the finest tea-shops in Kent that lie close to a convenient walk offering something by way of scenery, history, wildlife or art. I hope that you enjoy the walks and the teas. I have certainly enjoyed putting this book together and would like to thank the many local residents who have helped me with the task.

Tea and scones as served at the Mermaid's Locker tea-rooms in Sandwich, just beside the town hall.

Walk No. 1   Dover

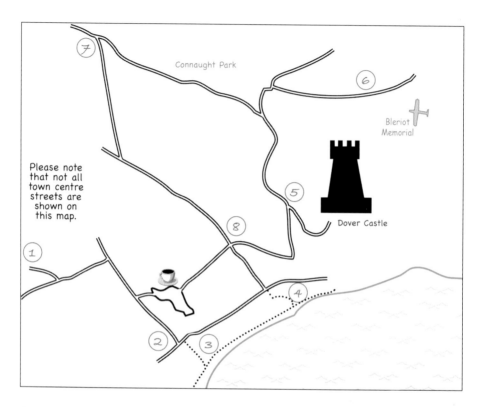

Connaught Park

6

Bleriot
Memorial

Please note
that not all
town centre
streets are
shown on
this map.

5

Dover Castle

7

1

8

4

2   3

The Bleriot Memorial marks the spot where the French pilot landed after becoming the first man to fly across the Channel.

1 Dover

Teashop:	**Dickens Corner Tea Rooms, 7 Market Sq, Dover, CT16 1LZ Tel: 01304 206692**
Distance:	**1.5 miles**
Map:	**OS Explorer 138**
Parking:	**There are several car parks in Dover.**
Public Transport:	**Dover is on the rail network**
Conditions:	**This walk is entirely over pavements. There are a couple of short but steepish hills.**

Since this short walk is around the ancient town centre of Dover, I have for once designed a walk that does not start and finish at the teashop. Instead it starts at the railway station and ends at the teashop. The reason for this is that the railway station is well signposted and easy to find. In a crowded town centre where car parking is difficult on most days I thought this made sense.

The Walk

Find Dover Priory Railway Station. This station was opened in 1861 to serve as a temporary terminal for the London, Dover and Chatham Railway line. It took the company six months to tunnel through the hill to Dover Harbour and erect a new terminus there. This station then became a passenger through station serving the town centre while the new stop became the main station for the docks and for passengers connecting to the cross-channel ferries - the famous "boat trains". Little of the 1861 station remains as it was almost entirely rebuilt in 1932, though that did give Dover an architectural classic of early 20th century design.

1) Leave the station along the access drive to reach Folkestone Road. Turn left. At a roundabout turn right into York Street.

2) Follow York Street to a second roundabout. Cross the main road and walk across the pedestrianised area to reach the seafront. To your right is the Dover Marina. To your left is the beach and seafront.

In the Marina you can catch a boat to take you out fishing on most days in the summer and irregularly in the spring and autumn. Although the Marina is for the use of private yachts and other small craft, it is part of the Port of Dover, which also includes the Eastern Docks - used by cross-channel ferries and other ships - and the largely disused Western Docks. On average Dover handles 16 million travellers, 700,000 trucks, 1.6 million cars and motorcycles and 118,000 buses each year, raising £15.5 billion a year and making this the busiest of the Channel ports.

There was a small port here in prehistoric times as the sheltered mouth of the River Dour (from which the town takes its name) was ideal for the small fishing craft and trading ships of the time. The Romans named the place Dubris and built a major naval base here. They built a lighthouse up on the hill where the medieval castle now stands, and that is still in pretty good condition - indeed it is the tallest Roman structure still standing in Britain. Not much else is left from Roman times due to the constant growth and redevelopment of the town and its fortifications over the centuries.

3) Turn left and walk along the seafront.

As you walk you will pass a statue of Matthew Webb, who on 24 August 1875 became the first man to swim the English Channel. He took a total of 21 hours and 45 minutes to get to France, after being stung by a jellyfish and caught in cross currents at Cap Gris Nez. There is also a statue of Charles Rolls (of Rolls-Royce fame) who in 1910 was the first man to fly across the Channel and back again without stopping.

4) After about 500 yards recross the main road and head inland along Maison Dieu Road (the A256). After about 150 yards turn right up the aptly named Castle Hill Road. You will find the entrance to Dover Castle on your right about halfway up.

The site has been fortified since Celtic times and was the site of a Roman outpost. In 1066 the invader William the Conqueror built a small wooden fortress on the hilltop to defend the port. It was not until the 1170s, however, that Dover Castle became a major fortress. The motives of King Henry II in massively rebuilding the small castle into one of the biggest

Dover Castle is one of the oldest in England.

fortresses in all Europe seems to have been prestige. He directed that all foreign dignitaries coming to England from Europe had to land at Dover and had to spend their first night on English soil in Dover Castle. This not only made the port of prime importance, but also gave the king a real motive in making the castle as impressive as possible.

Henry II built the Great Tower to serve as both a fortified base and as a luxurious stopping place for visitors. It has recently undergone a multi-million pound restoration that has seen the fabric repaired and the interior restored to its 12th century magnificence. During the summer months costumed staff recreate the medieval atmosphere.

By the 16th century the invention of cannon had made the medieval walls and towers obsolete. Henry VIII had the Moat Bulwark built as a gun platform. Thereafter the castle served mostly as a barracks and armoury until the outbreak of the Napoleonic Wars when it was converted again into a modern fortress. The Horseshoe, Hudson's, East Arrow and East Demi-Bastions were built to provide extra gun positions, and many other extensions and strongpoints were added. A network of secret tunnels was also installed. These came to the fore again in 1940 when, as a naval command base, they served as the administrative HQ for the Dunkirk Evacuation that saved the British army from the German panzers.

The castle is open year round. In the winter it is open 10 to 4 and in the summer from 10 to 6. The entrance fee is not cheap at £13.40, but there is enough to keep you busy all day. For the purposes of this walk it is recommended that you view the castle from the outside only and return another time to have a look around.

5) After viewing the Castle, or visiting it if you have the time, continue along Castle Hill Road to the junction on the right with Upper Road. Turn right. Follow Upper Road for about 400 yards to find the Bleriot Monument.

Louis Bleriot was a French engineer, born in 1872, who made a fortune from inventing the first workable motor car headlight. His passion, however, was flying. From 1895 he spent most of his time and income on building aircraft, most of which spectacularly failed to fly. Success came in 1907 with the Bleriot Mk V which flew well on several occasions before a gust of wind sent it crashing into the ground to utter destruction. Bleriot walked away from the wreck with a renewed appreciation of aerodynamics. In January 1909 he completed the Bleriot Mk XI.

The British newspaper the *Daily Express* had put up a prize of a thousand pounds to the first person to fly over the English Channel. On 19 July the pioneer airman Hubert Latham took off from Calais and was going well until his engine failed and he ditched just six miles from Dover. That left the field clear for Bleriot, who was recovering from an injury to his foot sustained in a crash earlier that year.

On 25 July Bleriot took off from Calais in his Mk XI. A French naval destroyer was waiting offshore in case he had to ditch. Bleriot soared to a height of 250 feet, adjusted the throttle to cruise at 40 miles per hour and settled down. He ran into a bank of unexpected cloud and feared that he had lost his way, but emerging on the far side he found Dover within sight. He headed for the open turf on the hill behind the castle and prepared to land. At the last minute a gust of wind sent his aircraft plunging down much faster than he intended. The undercarriage was smashed off and the aircraft came to a juddering halt. Bleriot was uninjured and clambered out to await the arrival of the crowds that had been watching his arrival on the seafront.

The path through the woods that leads to the Bleriot Memorial.

The Bleriot Memorial takes the form of a granite outline of the Mk XI in the turf where it came to rest.

6) Return along Upper Road to Castle Hill Road. Turn left and then right into Connaught Road. On your right is Connaught Park.

These fine gardens cover 30 acres. The land was donated by Queen Victoria and a public subscription raised to cover the costs of converting the wild woodland into a pleasure park. It was opened in 1883 by the Duke and Duchess of Connaught and has been maintained by the town Council ever since. The park is said to be haunted by a gent wearing a top hat.

7) Leaving the park, continue along Connaught Road to the junction with Park Avenue. Turn left into Park Avenue. At the bottom of the hill turn left into Maison Dieu Road and continue back to the junction with Castle Hill Road.

8) Turn right into Castle Street. You will find the teashop at the far end of this short road as it opens out into Market Square.

These fantastic tearooms are open from Monday to Saturday 8.30 to 4.30. They are closed on Sundays. This is one of the few tearooms that still offer a formal afternoon tea complete with cucumber sandwiches, dainties and cakes. Of course, it has an a la carte menu of cakes, scones and the like as well if you prefer a lighter option.

The Dickens Corner tearooms stand in the centre of Dover overlooking the pedestrianised market square.

Walk No. 2   Lenham

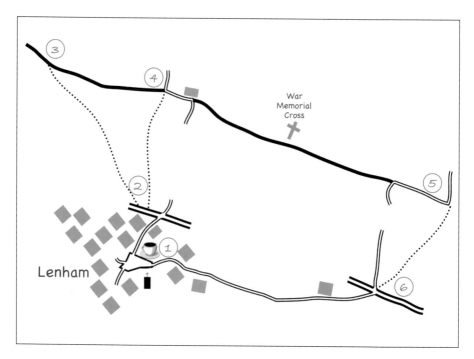

War
Memorial
Cross

Lenham

Pippa's tearooms in Lenham are housed in this ancient building on the village square.

2 Lenham

Teashop:	Pippa's Tea Rooms, Corner House, The Square, Lenham, Kent ME17 2PQ Tel: 01622 851360
Distance:	1.5 miles
Map:	OS Explorer 137
Parking:	There is limited car parking outside the teashop and a larger car park about 150 yards away.
Public Transport:	Lenham is on the rail network.
Conditions:	A short walk over firm going that includes a short stretch of the medieval Pilgrim's Way. There is one steep hill up and another down.

The Walk

1) The teashop is in The Square in the heart of the village. From the teashop walk northeast along Faversham Road to meet the Ashford Road, A20.

2) Cross the A20 with care. Then bear obliquely left up the slope of the hill in front of you. There are two paths. You really want the second of these, but the first will take you up to the same track along the hillside and gives a slightly shorter walk.

3) At the far end of the path it emerges on to a track. Whichever path you used, turn right. This is the Pilgrim's Way.

This long distance footpath links the two great medieval cathedrals of southern England: Winchester and Canterbury. Although it is named for the pilgrims who used this route to get between the two pilgrimage centres, it is actually a prehistoric trackway that was used for trade and travel long before the pilgrims came. The path was created in the days

At the top of the hill this sign indicates the route to be followed just beneath the crest of the hill.

before road building techniques were known. For most of its length it follows a route, as here, that is just below the crest of the hills. It therefore avoids both the heavily forested, damp and often boggy valley floors as well as the hilltops which are in many places overlain with a layer of clay which is slick after rain. Once proper road surfaces began to be built the valleys could be used and the Pilgrim's Way fell out of use as a major thoroughfare, thus preserving it as a long distance footpath.

4) Where the track meets a lane go straight on. When the lane turns sharp right, continue straight on along a new track, again the Pilgrim's Way.

On your left you will pass a huge cross hacked out of the chalk. This was first carved in 1922 as a war memorial to the local men who had been killed in the Great War of 1914-18. When war came again in 1939 the cross was filled in to stop its stark white outline being used as a navigational aid by the pilots of the Luftwaffe come to rain death and destruction on Britain. It was cleared after the Second World War ended, but was not fully restored until 1994 when it was rededicated to all local men who had died in both World Wars and other conflicts.

5) Where the track meets a lane continue straight on. When the lane bends left, turn sharp right to join a footpath heading back down the hill.

The Pilgrim's Way runs along the hillside north of the village.

6) When the path meets the A20 cross the main road with care. Then take the Old Ashford Road back to The Square and the teashop.

As you enter The Square you will see the Church of St Mary on your left. The first church here was built in about 950, it is mentioned in the Domesday Book, and was enlarged in Norman times. That church was deliberately burned down in 1297. Archbishop Robert Winchelsea of Canterbury came to Lenham in person to excommunicate the wicked fellow who started the blaze, but he had fled. Undeterred, the archbishop excommunicated him anyway. The church seen today is the structure put up to replace the lost original. A column between the Chancel and Chapel is thought to be the only recognisable bit of the old church still in place, though no

The great chalk cross on the hill above Lenham that serves as a war memorial for the village.

doubt many stones were reused. The pulpit is of late Tudor date and is one of the finest in Kent. The nave retains its 18th century box pews. The ring of 8 bells is reckoned to be one of the most melodic in southern England.

Pippa's Tea Rooms are in a most attractive setting overlooking the village square. All food is freshly prepared and has a good selection of toasted sandwiches, jacket potatoes and special dishes of the day.

Walk No. 3   Hernhill

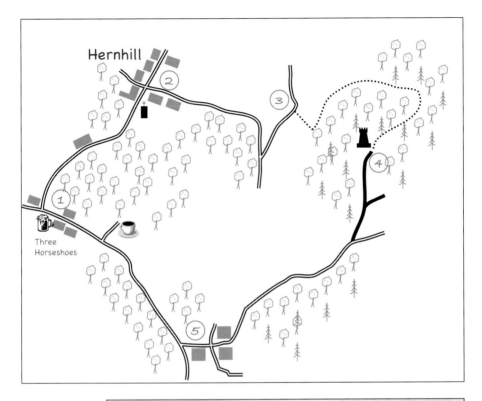

The Red Lion in Hernhill overlooks the Green and marks the spot where this walk turns right off the lane.

3 Hernhill

Teashop:	The Woodrose Restaurant and Tea Garden, Mount Ephraim, Staplestreet Road, Hernhill, Kent ME13 9TX Tel: 01227 751168
Distance:	3 miles
Map:	OS Explorer 149
Parking:	The teashop has a car park. Check for opening times.
Public Transport:	Boughton Street is on Stagecoach bus route 3A from Canterbury. The teashop is about a 10 minute walk from the bus stop.
Conditions:	This walk is short but strenuous as it goes up and down steep hills that offer fine views.

The Walk

1) Leave the teashop and return to Staplestreet Road. Turn right and head northwest. When you reach the Three Horseshoes pub turn right along Church Hill. As you enter the village of Hernhill you will find a church on your right.

The little village of Hernhill had one of the earlier churches in Kent, it was certainly here by about 750. That early structure was of wood and in 1120 was replaced by a stone and timber structure that was dedicated to St Stephen, as the first church may have been. In 1450 the church was demolished and replaced with the stone and flint building that is to be seen today. Unusually the dedication was changed to St Michael, though no reason for this is known.

The church at Hernhill is a fine example of the unique style of Perpendicular Gothic that prevailed in Kent during the 15th century.

The church is a fine example of Kent Perpendicular Gothic style and has a square tower with a ring of eight bells. The main door and door to the bell tower are 15th century, and the rood screen is 16th century. Much of the furniture dates from a restoration of the church in the 19th century, and a Lady Chapel was added in 1928 - though in a very sympathetic style that does not jar with the rest of the church.

2) Pass the church on your right then turn right down Crockham Lane. Ignore the first on the right and instead take the first on the left, a lane which cuts back uphill.

3) After about 300 yards the lane bends to the left. At this point take a footpath off to the right that climbs uphill toward woodland. In the woods, the path bends sharp left, then hooks right to complete a half circle and emerges on to a track. In the woods to the right stands a semi-derelict tower.

This is the Holly Hill Tower. It was built by the local landowner in the 1930s, apparently so that he could enjoy the views north towards the Thames Estuary and its ships. It has been abandoned since his death and is now rather run down. It is not open to the public, but is an interesting example of a very late example of a folly.

4) From the tower follow the track south until it emerges on to a lane. Turn right along this lane, Dawes Road, to a skewed crossroads junction. Go straight on along Dawes Road to a T-junction.

5) Turn right into Staplestreet Road and return to the tearooms.

The view from the upper slopes of Holly Hill back towards Hernhill. The church tower can be seen to the right and the brick facade of Mount Ephraim on the left.

The old beacon that stands on Holly Hill overlooking the Thames Estuary about four miles to the north.

Walk No. 4   Walmer

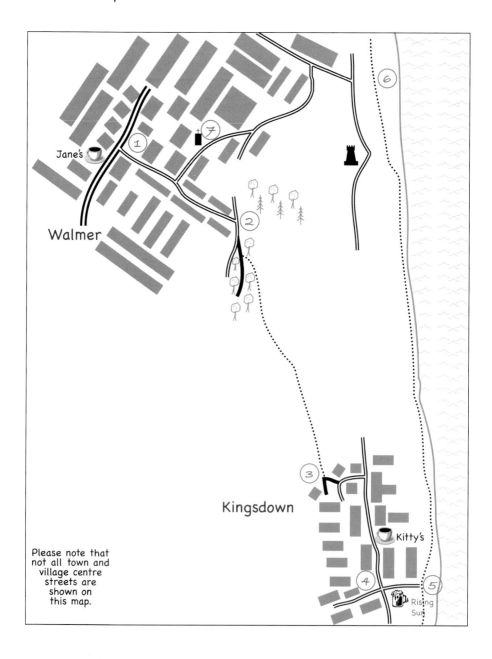

Jane's

Walmer

Kingsdown

Kitty's

Please note that
not all town and
village centre
streets are
shown on
this map.

Rising
Sun

4 Walmer

Teashop:	Jane's Tea Rooms, 323, Dover Rd, Walmer, Deal, Kent CT14 7NX Tel: 01304 365553
Distance:	4 miles
Map:	OS Explorer 150
Parking:	There is on-street parking near the teashop and a car park beside the castle.
Public Transport:	Walmer is on the rail network.
Conditions:	This walk is mostly over surfaced paths. It takes in 2 miles of coastline and Walmer Castle.

There are two teashops on this walk and both are good, offering excellent home-baked cakes and a lovely refreshing cup of tea. I have chosen to start and finish the walk at Jane's for the simple reason that it is open six days a week, while Kitty's (excellent though it is) is open only four days a week.

The Walk

1) Leave Jane's and walk north along Dover Road for about 100 yards. Turn right into Gram's Road.

2) At the far end of Gram's Road turn right into Liverpool Road. Almost at once veer left through a car park and on to a track that passes through woodland. This track divides almost as soon as it leaves the small car park. Take the right hand fork. Follow the track for a couple of hundred yards through woodland until it emerges on to a green. Veer left onto a footpath

A selection of the fine individual cakes baked at Jane's Tea Rooms.

The houses that line the beach at Kingsdown. The walk runs along the beach, but a surfaced path between the houses and beach makes for easier walking.

that strikes off over the grassy open ground and then beside a hedge around the shoulder of Hawks Hill, with the hilltop to your right.

3) This path eventually passes through a clump of bushes to reach a track. Turn left and follow the track to a small residential road. Continue straight on along the road to a T-junction with Kingsdown Road.

4) Turn right along Kingsdown Road to a crossroads by the Rising Sun pub. Turn left along South Road. At the far end of South Road you will find a car parking area, beyond which is the beach and the sea.

If you look to your right, you will see the land rising steeply upward. This is the northern end of the famous White Cliffs that march away south towards and beyond Dover, stretching into Sussex. There is a footpath up on to the cliff top, but it traverses the rifle ranges used by the Royal Marines and is often closed to walkers.

5) Turn left to walk north along the beach. After about a mile and a half the impressive bulk of Walmer Castle will come into sight on the left.

It was somewhere here, nobody is entirely certain where, that the Roman legions of Julius Caesar landed in 55BC on his preliminary raid into Britain. Caesar had been busy that year, having already crossed the Rhine to intimidate the German tribes into a peace treaty. Caesar claimed that while his back was turned agents from Celtic tribes in Britain had been trying to stir up trouble among the Celtic peoples of Gaul (now France), then part of the Roman empire. In response Caesar decided to land a force in Britain as a show of strength. It is unlikely he intended anything more serious as it was by this time late in the summer and campaigning would have had to stop in a few weeks time.

With a fleet of about 100 ships, most of them commandeered merchantmen, Caesar headed for Dover. The small port there was well known to Roman merchants, but it was defended and Caesar did not fancy his chances of getting ashore safely. He therefore headed north along the coast. A short distance beyond the end of the cliffs, Caesar reckoned that the open beach was a good place to put his men ashore.

Unfortunately as the ships nosed into the shallows a force of British cavalry came galloping down the hills from the south. They had apparently ridden north from Dover, following the ships. Behind the cavalry came chariots and, Caesar assumed, some distance behind them were the British infantry hurrying to catch up. The enemy horsemen came down to the beach and began hurling javelins at any Roman soldier who came too close. Understandably, the legionaries hung back.

Then the standard bearer of the 10th legion pushed his way through the throng and the surf. He turned his back contemptuously on the British and shouted to his comrades "Follow me, fellow soldiers, unless you wish to betray your eagle to the enemy. I, for my part, will perform my duty to the republic and to my general." He then charged the beach, followed

The beach north of Kingsdown where Julius Caesar and the Roman legions landed in 55BC.

by the legionaries. The beach was quickly cleared and a defended camp hurriedly thrown up before the British infantry could arrive.

The campaign then became a series of skirmishes and small battles with neither side willing to take any risks. As the autumn storms closed in, Caesar shipped his men back to Gaul. He would return the following year to enjoy rather more success. In 54BC he won a great battle, probably at what is now known as Bigbury Camp in Kent, and forced the tribes of southern Britain to pay tribute to Rome. Once again, Caesar did not remain permanently and it would be another hundred years before the Romans came to stay.

Walmer Castle has nothing to do with that ancient battle, though it may stand very close to the site of Caesar's temporary fort. It was, in fact, built on the orders of King Henry VIII in 1539 at a time when a French invasion was feared. It was one of three forts constructed to defend The Downs, an area of safe anchorage just off the coast here that is protected by the Goodwin Sands. The other forts were at Deal and Sandown, a short distance to the north.

The forts were all designed to mount artillery and to be proof against both modern cannon and up-to-date siege techniques. They were state of the art military installations for their time. At the centre of Walmer Castle is a circular keep. Cannon were mounted on the roof of the keep, which had massively thick stone walls to withstand incoming cannonballs. Around the keep was a courtyard, beyond which were four massive semi-circular bastions. Like the keep these mounted heavy guns and had astonishingly thick walls. In all Walmer could mount 39 big guns.

The entire fort was sunk into the ground so that none of the walls stood up to present an easy target to an enemy gunner. Around the fort is a deep, wide ditch or dry moat with sheer walls on both sides. Any attacking infantry would need to climb down into the moat and then up the other side if they were to enter the castle. Around the base of the interior wall is a series of loopholes through which the defenders could mow down the attackers. The prospect of an assault was virtually suicidal. Only a prolonged barrage of heavy guns could hope to have much impact, and even then starvation was probably a more realistic option for an attacker.

In 1708 Walmer Castle was designated as the official residence of the Warden of the Cinque Ports. This position dated back to the 13th century and was originally a very important naval command. The Cinque Ports - Hastings, New Romney, Hythe, Dover and Sandwich, plus the two "ancient towns" of Rye and Winchelsea - had a key role in supplying ships to the King of England in time of war. Most of these were merchant ships adapted for war use, a perfectly adequate procedure in the days before gunpowder. Later on the founding of the Royal Navy and the development of naval gunnery made converted merchant ships less useful and by 1630 the Cinque Ports had lost their naval importance, though they continued to be busy merchant ports.

The post of Warden had therefore become one with few duties but good pay. It was used as a way of rewarding a person who had performed well for the monarch. Among those to have held the position have been the Duke of Wellington, Winston Churchill and Sir Robert Menzies. The castle is still used for formal functions, but mostly houses a museum dedicated to the Cinque Ports. The room where Wellington died is preserved as it was on that fatal day.

6) Having viewed the castle, and visited if time permitted, continue north along the seafront for about 200 yards. Turn left into Granville Road. After about 150 yards turn left into Liverpool Road. After 200 yards bear right into St Clare Road to find St Mary's Church on your right.

This church was designed by Arthur Blomfield in 1887 to take the pressure off the parish's two other churches, both of which were in origin private chapels and of a suitably small size. The entrance is a three-bay baptistery, into a tall clerestoried nave with narrow aisles either side. The main west window portrays nautical episodes of Christ's life such as the miraculous draught of fishes, preaching from the boat and calming the storm. There are other fine windows and the rood screen is a particularly impressive piece of Victorian Gothic.

7) After viewing the church continue along St Clare Road to a T-junction. Turn right along Gram's Road and so return to Jane's.

Jane's is open Monday to Saturday 10 to 5 year round. It is a baker's shop with a tearoom attached so you can buy bread or cakes to take home if you wish. Kitty's is open Thursday to Sunday 11am to 4.30pm. On Sundays Kitty's serves a magnificent roast lunch - but you will need to book in advance as it is very popular and tends to get booked up.

Walmer Castle is the official residence of the Warden of the Cinque Ports and is open to the public.

Walk No. 5   West Malling

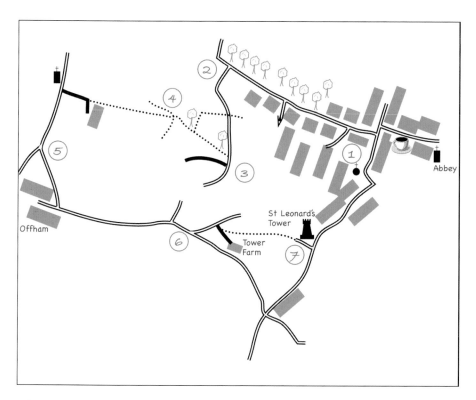

The High Street at West Malling is one of the widest in Kent.

5 West Malling

Teashop:	The Old Mill Tea Room Ltd, Mill Yard Craft Centre, Swan St, West Malling, Kent ME19 6LP Tel: 01732 844311
Distance:	4 miles
Map:	OS Explorer 148
Parking:	There is on-street parking near the teashop
Public Transport:	West Malling is on the rail network
Conditions:	This walk is a gentle walk through orchards and past a ruined medieval castle.

Squeezed between the A20 and the A228, and with both the railway and the M20 less than a mile to the north, it might be thought that West Malling would be a noisy, modern place. This could not be further from the truth. Indeed, the village is one of the most historic in Kent and can be a remarkably peaceful and charming spot.

The Walk

1) The walk starts at the parish church of St Mary.

If this church looks familiar, that is no wonder. This is the church that featured on the back of the Bank of England ten pound note from 1994 to 2003. The reason it was there is that it formed the backdrop to the cricket match scene from the *Pickwick Papers*, the author of which - Charles Dickens - was on the front of the note.

Having viewed the church and green, walk north along the High Street. Turn left down West Street. This street becomes Norman Road as it leaves the village.

An overgrown tomb in the churchyard at Offham.

2) Just before Norman Road turns sharp right to go under the railway turn left down Fartherwell Road.

3) About 300 yards along Fartherwell Road a footpath crosses over the road. Turn right up the signposted path, climbing a series of eroded steps to reach a field on top of a bank. The footpath will jink sharp left, then run alongside a wood to turn right again and so reach an asymmetrical 5-way junction of tracks and footpaths.

4) Continue straight on across the fields toward Godwell Farm. At the farm continue on along a track that takes you to Church Farm. Up the lane to the right you will see a church.

Although this church dedicated to St Michael is rather on its own, it is the parish church of Offham, which lies half a mile to the south. The church was founded in 832 as a wooden structure, but rebuilt in stone in about 1080. Only the lower courses of these ancient walls remain as the church has been renovated and restored several times. The church is usually locked, but the keys are held at the adjacent farm and if the farmer is in he will happily lend you the key. The interior is whitewashed, but otherwise is typically medieval.

5) Walk south along Church Road to a Y-junction. Bear left, then at a T-junction turn right and walk about 150 yards to find the village green on your left.

The quintain at Offham is a rare medieval survivor, a nearby inscribed stone explains the uses to which this object was put.

On the green you will see a quintain. This is often claimed to be the original medieval quintain and thus to be only the quintain in its original position. Hopefully this is the case, but some suspect that the quintain may have been so updated and repaired over the centuries that little of the original remains. The quintain was removed during the summer of 1940 because it featured in many tourist guidebooks to England published in Germany. It was feared that if the German invasion that was then expected should take place, the incoming Nazi hordes would be equipped with these books to help them navigate around the countryside. The quintain was so distinctive that it would at once have told the Germans where they were, and so it was removed for safekeeping.

6) After viewing the quintain and adjacent carved stone, retrace your steps to the east. Follow this road to a Y-junction and bear left. After about 200 yards the track to Tower Farm

turns off right. Adjacent to the track is a footpath that cuts across the fields and over the crest of a hill towards the distant St Leonard's Tower.

St Leonard's Tower is a surprisingly massive ruined castle tower to find in a quiet little place like West Malling - but it is the wreck of what was once an even larger fortress built here by Bishop Gundulf of Rochester in 1080. The fortress was the result of a behind-closed-doors deal between Duke William of Normandy and Pope Alexander II in 1065.

At the time King Edward the Confessor of England was old, ill and dying - and he had no children. The succession was obviously going to be disputed and Duke William reckoned he was in with a chance. His claim was weak, based as it was on a

The path that leads from the track to Tower Farm to St Leonard's Tower runs between two fences.

relationship by marriage, and certainly weaker than that of Earl Harold of Wessex who was the grandson of a former king of England. To try to shore up his claim, William promised Pope Alexander that, if he became king, he would hand power over the Church in England to Alexander. At the time the English Church was a semi-independent organisation that followed some rules of its own - clergy were allowed to marry for instance - and which did not pay as much cash to Rome as Alexander thought it should. In response, Alexander issued a ruling that William was the legitimate King of England and sent him a banner that had been sprinkled with holy water by the Pope himself in St Peter's Basilica, Rome.

After William won the Battle of Hastings in 1066, killed Harold and became king, he was as good as his word. He sacked Archbishop Stigand of Canterbury and put in his place a papal placeman named Lanfranc. As soon as he was secure in his post, Lanfanc sent for other foreigners to occupy the senior positions in the English church in order to enforce the unpopular reforms and taxes on the natives. One of these was Gundulf, who arrived in 1070 and became Bishop of Rochester in 1075.

Gundulf's first move was to begin rebuilding the cathedral at Rochester in suitably foreign style, but soon had to look to his safety, which was why he began building a series of castles across his diocese. West Malling Castle was the greatest of these. The remaining tower was the central keep, or most formidable tower, in the fortress. Today it stands 60 feet tall but was originally a full storey taller, topped by battlements and at least one turret. The building remained in use throughout the Middle Ages as a fortress-residence of the Bishops of Rochester, but was later converted to use as a prison. It was then sold into private hands and was used for a variety of purposes, such as a hop store and quarry for building stone until it reached its current ruined condition.

7) Continue down the footpath to meet a road. Turn left to walk back into West Malling. To find the Old Mill Tea Room, continue past the church and then turn right down Swan Street. The tearooms are on the right after about 50 yards.

If you have time you might care to continue along Swan Street to find the Abbey ruins.

The West Malling Abbey, or more properly the Abbey of St Mary was a home for Benedictine nuns. The abbey was given the right to pasture domestic animals in nearby royal forests, but more lucrative was the right to hold a weekly market for local farmers and an annual fair for international merchants. The Malling Market was to become famous, bringing in huge amounts of cash in the form of a commission charged on everything sold. What had been a little village grew into a flourishing market town. The Abbey grew as well and by 1500 was in the top 30% of religious houses in terms of profits from its estates.

In the course of the Protestant Reformation of King Henry VIII, Malling Abbey was one of the religious houses earmarked for closure in 1538. The royal officials came from London, armed with the standard documents which the Abbess was required to sign, handing over

St Leonard's Tower was designed by the same man responsible for the White Tower at the Tower of London.

the care of the Abbey and its estates to the king who was by then head of the Church of England and so, in theory at least, owned the lands anyway. Abbess Margaret Vernon refused to sign. Nor could any of her nuns be found willing to sign on her behalf. This was a unique event in the Dissolution of the Monasteries. Most of the ousted monks and nuns were only too happy to sign the documents in return for a personal pension and the promise that a proportion of the estates would be used for charitable purposes. The Malling Nuns refused and so became heroines to those who opposed the Reformation.

It made little difference. Henry VIII took the abbey anyway and sold it into private hands. The Abbey then fell into disrepair as houses, barns and workshops were built on the site and out of its stones. Today the great Norman tower remains along with fragments

The walk leaves Fartherwell Road here to climb the worn steps to run along the edge of a field at the top of this bank.

of the transepts and one side of the nave. The ruins and the buildings among them are now in the care of a community of Anglican Benedictine nuns who have been here since 1906.

The Old Mill Tea Rooms are open Monday to Saturday 9.30 to 4.30 throughout the year. On Sundays they are open only if there is some local event going on, so phone before you set off if you want to call on a Sunday. They make their own cakes (which are delicious) and serve light lunches from noon until 3pm upstairs in winter outside tables in summer.

Walk No. 6 — Penshurst

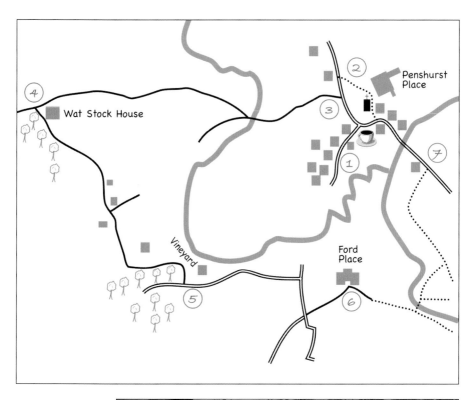

The unique lychgate that runs under the upper floor of a house to carry this walk from the High Street into the churchyard at Penshurst.

6 Penshurst

Teashop:	Quaintways Tea Rooms, High St, Penshurst, Tonbridge, Kent TN11 8BT Tel: 01892 870272
Distance:	4 miles
Map:	OS Explorer 147
Parking:	There is a car park in Fordcombe Road in the village.
Public Transport:	Penshurst is on the rail network
Conditions:	This walk is a hilly route through woodland and past Penshurst Place.

The Walk

1) Find the car park on the southwestern edge of the village in Fordcombe Road, the B2188. On exiting the car park turn right to head north along Fordcombe Road. At a T-junction with the B2176, Penshurst Road, turn right. You will pass Quaintways Tea Rooms on your right. After about 50 yards turn left to enter the churchyard through perhaps the most unusual lychgate in England.

It is not the gate itself that is odd, but the fact that some time around 1550 a local man decided to build his home up and around the gate. The house is still there, complete with gnarled oak timbers, bulging walls and sagging roof. It forms a weird form of domestic arch over the lychgate.

Once through the gate you will find yourself in the churchyard of the Church of St John the Baptist, the four towering pinnacles of which make this the tallest building for miles around. The church was begun in the 12th century, and then saw assorted

The hanging kettle that is displayed outside the Quaintways Tea Rooms in Penshurst.

The North Front of Penshurst Place is of Tudor date, but parts of the house go back to 1340.

enlargements and alterations in the 13th, 14th and 15th centuries. Then in the early 19th century the Sidney Family added a small private chapel and paid for the entire church to be restored, renovated and generally rebuilt. The result of all this work is a strangely pleasing hotchpotch of styles and materials. One of the more interesting features is a magnificent window of 1620, again paid for by the Sidney family.

2) On the far side of the churchyard the footpath crosses a field. Penshurst Place is on your right. If you have the time to spare you could visit this stately home.

Penshurst Place has been the home of the Sidney family who did so much for the local church since 1552. The earliest of the Sidneys to achieve acclaim was Sir Philip Sidney. This elegant courtier and artist achieved fame with his sonnets, short poems and longer works on a variety of themes. He went on to write the *Arcadia*, which in its day outsold Shakespeare, Marlow and other writers. He also wrote *The Defence of Poesie*, a riposte to the growing fashion for stage plays.

In 1572 Sidney chanced to be in Paris when the horrific St Bartholomew's Day Massacre took place. He managed to save himself from the Catholic murder squads, which butchered an estimated 30,000 Protestants over a six day period, by seeking refuge in the home of the English ambassador. Other Protestants were not so lucky and were cut down even as they reached the steps of the house. The brutality of the event changed Sidney. He still wrote poetry, but spent rather more time on military campaigns. He joined the Dutch Protestant rebels fighting against the Catholic monarch Philip II of Spain. In 1586 he was badly wounded fighting in the Battle of Zutphen, but famously handed his water bottle to a wounded comrade saying "Thy necessity is yet greater than mine". He died a few days later.

The Sidney family, meanwhile, prospered. They later rose to be Earls of Leicester, but when the direct male line died out so did the title. The Sidneys are today the Barons de l'Isle and Dudley. The great house in which they live began as a fairly modest manor house in 1340, some parts of which remain. The Hall, for instance, is reckoned the finest medieval feasting hall to survive virtually unaltered anywhere in Britain. The house was extensively rebuilt in

Tudor times and it is this which forms most of Penshurst Place as it stands today. The house contains a magnificent collection of table services and of arms and armour - including the helmet Sir Philip was wearing when he received his death wound.

The house and gardens are open daily from early April to late October. At other times of the year you should check opening times on their website www.penshurstplace.com/ or by phoning them on 01892 870307.

3) Continue along the footpath until it reaches the B2176. Turn left and then almost immediately right along a bridleway. Where this bridleway crosses a stream by way of a bridge it meets a Y-junction. Take the right hand branch up a hill.

4) As the track enters woodland, turn left along a track that leaves the woodland and then goes downhill to pass some houses, jink left along the edge of some woodland and then bear right to emerge on to a lane. At the lane turn left.

On your left are the Penshurst Vineyards where some excellent wines are produced.

5) Continue along the lane to a T-junction with the B2188. Turn right, then at a crossroads left up a track to Ford Place.

6) At Ford Place bear right across open fields. When this path meets a stream there is a Y-junction. Turn left over a footbridge and then at a second junction turn left along a path that becomes a track and emerges onto the B2176 at Elliott's Farm.

7) Turn left to return to Penshurst. Quaintways Tea Rooms will be on your left after you pass the church.

Quaintways is open in the summer months on Tuesday to Friday from 10 to 5, and on weekends 10 to 5.30. In the winter months they are open Tuesday to Sunday 10 to 5. A formal set afternoon tea is available in the summer.

The River Eden as seen from the bridge that carries the track leading from Penshurst to Wat Stock.

Walk No. 7   Otford

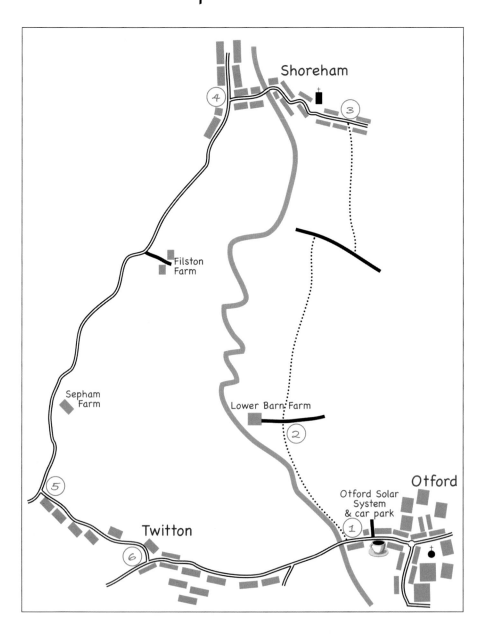

7 Otford

Teashop:	Hospices of Hope Otford Tea Shop, 11a High St, Otford, Sevenoaks, TN14 5PG Tel: 01959 524322
Distance:	4 miles
Map:	OS Explorer 147
Parking:	There is on-street parking around the village green.
Public Transport:	Otford is on the rail network
Conditions:	This walk is over fairly level ground, so the going is generally easy. However, the early stages cross riverside meadows and can be muddy after rain.

This walk starts in the High Street car park, just a couple of doors along from the teashop. Before leaving the car park it is worth taking the time to view the famous Otford Solar System, built in 2000 as a project to mark the Millennium. The monument is a scale model of the real solar system on a scale of about 1:4.5 billion. The Sun is represented by a brass dome mounted on a stone pillar in the recreation ground. The planets Mercury, Venus, Earth and Mars are also marked by pillars in the recreation ground. The more

The tearooms in Otford share premises with a charity shop.

distant planets of Jupiter, Saturn, Neptune, Uranus and Pluto are indicated by pillars elsewhere around the village and are linked by a marked walk - it takes about 45 minutes if you are feeling energetic enough. They are not part of this walk, but feel free to do it if you like.

The Walk

1) From the car park in the High Street head west along High Street. Immediately before the bridge over the River Darent turn right along a footpath signed as being the Darent

The Otford Solar System is formed by a number of stone pillars, one for each of the major objects in the solar system. This photo shows the Sun in the foreground with the Earth beyond.

Valley Path, one of several long-distance footpaths in Kent.

Although the river has been deepened, channelled and the surrounding meadows drained over the years, it is fairly certain that it was at this spot that the great Battle of Otford was fought in the year 776.

At this date what is now England was divided into a number of different kingdoms, some more powerful than others. Kent had always been relatively rich, but it was small and by 776 was under the domination of King Offa of Mercia. The exact nature of this overlordship is unclear, but a dispute broke out when King Egbert of Kent granted some royal lands to the Bishop of Rochester without asking Offa's permission first. There then followed further quarrels, the details of which have not been recorded. In the spring of 776 Offa seems to have had enough. He sent Egbert an ultimatum that was refused. War broke out.

Offa mustered the Mercian army and sent it marching to London. In Canterbury people saw a vision of Christ's cross in the sky bathed in blood. Nobody knew what it meant, but it cannot have been good news. Archbishop Janbert announced that he had studied the details of the dispute and decided that Egbert was in the right. Offa ignored him.

The Mercian army passed over London bridge without incident, then swung southeast to enter Kent by crossing the River Darent at the ford at Otford. The reason why the Mercians had to use a bridge or ford was because of their supply train. At this date an English army would have carried with them a fair amount of camping equipment, cooking gear, food and spare weaponry. The baggage would not have been as cumbersome as it would become later, but even so an army would have needed a large number of pack horses, ox carts and the like.

Offa did not march with his army, he seems to have sent only a part of the force that Mercia could muster – perhaps around 3,000 men or so. Even so the army of Kent would have been seriously outnumbered. It would have made sense to Egbert to try to halt the invasion at a bottleneck in the supply system, and so he came to the ford at Otford.

At this date, the fighting men of both sides would have been infantry - though some may have ridden on ponies when on the march. They were equipped with shield, spear and a sidearm such as a knife or axe. Only the richer men would have had coats of mail or metal helmets. Most men had two or more lightweight javelins as well as their heavy, thrusting

An autumnal mist creeps up the valley of the Darent with the North Downs beyond, as seen from Otford.

spear. These would be thrown towards the enemy in the opening stages of a battle.

The main tactic at the time was the shield wall. This involved the front ranks closing up and locking shields to produce a solid wall. The rest of the men formed up six or so ranks deep behind. This solid mass of men would then advance on the enemy. It was usual to place the more experienced men at the front to ensure that the face of the formation remained tightly knit and as straight as possible. It is thought that formations usually advanced at a trot so as to combine momentum with the ability to keep formation - though some forces of veterans could run. Once the two sides were locked in combat, it was a matter of spear thrusts and counter thrusts to kill and injure the opposition. Eventually one side or other would begin to lose formation, and often the shield wall broke up completely as an army turned in rout.

Egbert and his men presumably lined the eastern bank of the Darent in shield wall formation. This would have forced the Mercians to splash over the river in order to get to grips, no doubt losing a lot of cohesion in their formation as they did so. It is possible that Egbert held his men back from the ford, luring the Mercians to start crossing, then attacking when the enemy was disordered. Either way the fiercest fighting would have raged about here.

Whatever happened, the battle ended in a stunning victory for the outnumbered Kentish army. The Mercians were chased back to London in defeat. Egbert had won complete independence for Kent and enjoyed that status for the rest of his life.

2) Continue straight across the track that leads to Lower Barn Farm and continue across the meadows. At a second track turn right, then left to continue along the Darent Valley Path as it weaves across the Darent Valley Golf Course.

3) When the path emerges on to a lane, Station Road, turn left into Shoreham village.

The pub at Shoreham stands opposite the church and offers fine lunches if you want one.

Shoreham was mentioned in the Domesday Book so was probably here when the battle was fought at Otford. If you look at the hillside ahead of you as you enter the village you should see a large white cross hacked into the turf of the hillside. This was carved in 1920 as a war memorial to honour the men of the village killed during the First World War. The cross is nowadays visible from the road only in winter as in summer the leaves on the trees block it from view. If you are doing this walk in summer you will need to find the village hall and go round the back to get a view.

As you enter the village you will pass the Church of St Peter and St Paul set back to your right on a corner. Rather unusually this is of brick and flint construction. Just beyond the church you will pass over the bridge across the Darent, also of brick and flint. This bridge forms the finish line for the Shoreham Duck Race, held on May Bank Holiday every year. The ducks may be simple shop-bought bath toys or elaborate home-made creations. There is a prize for the best looking duck and another for the first duck to reach this bridge out of the hundreds released some distance upstream. All money raised goes to local charities.

Shoreham is perhaps best known for the Shoreham Aircraft Museum, which is well signposted if you fancy visiting. The museum was opened in 1978 to commemorate the Battle of Britain that was fought in the skies overhead in 1940. It contains hundreds of aviation relics from crashed British and German aircraft excavated from nearby fields, as well as items which have been kindly donated. In addition, there is a fine collection of flying helmets, uniforms and insignia. This, along with a comprehensive display of Home Front memorabilia, ensures a visit to the museum is both enjoyable and educational. The museum is staffed by volunteers and so is open only on summer weekends and Bank Holiday Mondays. Details are available on the museum's website www.shoreham-aircraft-museum.co.uk.

4) At a T-junction turn left into Filston Lane. Follow this lane out of the village and through fields for about a mile and a half. Note that if you want to find the village hall to see the Cross you will need to turn right to find the hall on your left after about 100 yards

5) Immediately before the lane crosses over a railway bridge, turn left into Twitton Lane.

6) Follow Twitton Lane to a T-junction. Turn left to follow this lane through Twitton and over the Darent back into Otford. The teashop will be on your right, sharing premises with a charity shop.

The teashop is open in the summer months Monday to Friday from 10 to 4.30 and to 5 on Saturday. In the winter it closes at 4. It is closed on Sunday.

If you continue past the teashop and turn right at the village green you will find the remains of the old Bishop's Palace on your left. It stands behind a large hedge, which you will have to walk past to find the entrance. Parts of what was once a huge rambling structure spread over 4 acres have been converted into private houses, other parts have fallen into ruin. There had been a residence of the bishops here since at least 900. The present structure was erected in 1515 by Archbishop Warham but was abandoned by the Church within a century and sold into private hands.

The ruined gatehouse of the Bishop's Palace at Otford lies south of the village pond.

Walk No. 8   Hadlow

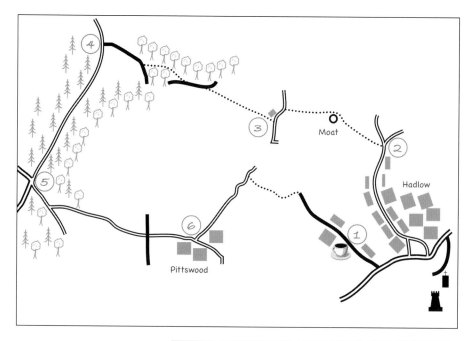

The walk leaves the road north of Hadlow by way of this broken kissing gate to run along the edge of a field heading west.

8 Hadlow

Teashop:	Hadlow College Tea Rooms, Tonbridge Rd, Hadlow, Tonbridge, Kent TN11 0AL Tel: 01732 853286
Distance:	4.5 miles
Map:	OS Explorer 136 and 148
Parking:	The tearooms have their own car park
Public Transport:	Hadlow is on Arriva bus route 7 from Tonbridge
Conditions:	This walk is through woodland that includes a couple of steep scrambles.

The Hadlow College Tea Rooms are on the premises of a garden centre, so don't be put off when trying to find them. They are well worth the finding - especially for their magnificent array of home-made cakes. Hadlow College of Agriculture and Horticulture was established in 1968. It is now one of the premier agricultural colleges in the country having branched out into fisheries management, garden design and other disciplines.

The Walk

1) Leave the tearooms and walk southeast to the A26 Tonbridge Road. Turn left along the main road to walk into the village of Hadlow itself. Continue for about 200 yards and then turn right into Church Street to visit the church and view the stunning Hadlow Tower.

Hadlow Church was built in 975, though only a few fragments of

The famous Hadlow Tower lost its top 40 feet after storm damage during the Great Storm of 1987 and is now awaiting repairs estimated to cost around three million pounds.

that first structure remain above ground today. The tower you see now was built in about 1220 and most of the rest of the church was erected over the following 150 years, and was renovated in 1636 - the date of this work is inscribed over the main door.

During the 13th century the church and manor of Hadlow were donated to the Knights Hospitaller. In origin a religious brotherhood dedicated to caring for sick pilgrims travelling to Jerusalem, the Hospitallers soon acquired a military wing which fought valiantly in the Crusades. The knights were distinguished by wearing a surcoat of red emblazoned with a white cross - the design still forms the flag of the order. The rents from villages such as Hadlow went to pay the considerable costs of campaigning against the Moslems in the Middle East and of maintaining hospitals for sick pilgrims.

When the Reformation came, the Knights Hospitaller were among the few religious orders not to be suppressed in England. They did, however, have all their property confiscated and survived in fragmentary form until they were refounded in 1831, gaining a formal Royal Charter in 1888. The order had survived in more complete form in other countries and is today a truly international order. The Knights Hospitaller

A Victoria sandwich cake on offer at the tearooms in Hadlow.

are today best known for their medical branch, the St John's Ambulance.

Just south of the church is the astonishing Hadlow Tower, sometimes called Hadlow Castle. The "Castle" is in reality an 18th century manor with a few crenelations to add a false medieval atmosphere. The remaining neo-Gothic Tower dominates the valley around Tonbridge and has many unique features. The Tower was completed in 1838 on the orders of the wealthy industrialist Walter Barton May, who then occupied Hadlow Castle. It is a fine example of neo-Gothic ecclesiastical architecture which was so favoured in the Victorian era. There are seven floors, each on an octagonal plan. The building is a private property and is not open to the public, but the exterior can be seen and is stunning. The Tower is now owned by Tonbridge Council, which has gained a Lottery Grant to help with the cost of restoring this structure to its former glory.

2) Having viewed the church and tower, return to the main road and turn left. Then turn right along Carpenters Lane. Follow this lane for about 700 yards to a Y-junction with Steers Place. Where Steers Place goes right and Carpenters Lane bears left, you need to join a footpath striking off sharp left over the open fields.

As you walk over the fields, you will find the path passes close by an old abandoned moat. It is usually assumed that this marks the site of a medieval residence of some kind, but no excavations have ever been carried out so nothing can be said for certain.

3) When the path emerges on to a lane, turn left. After passing a house on the right, join a new path continuing westwards towards some woods about 800 yards away. At the edge of the wood the path joins a track for a while, then veers off the track to the right to plunge through the woods, pass a small pond on the right and then join a second track which heads east to a lane, Puttenden Road, beside a second pond.

A coffee layer cake, slices of which can be bought at the tearooms in Hadlow.

4) Turn left along Puttenden Road. Follow this fairly straight lane through woodland to a junction with the A227 and Higham Lane.

5) Turn left along Higham Lane, and then left again into Ashes Lane.

6) At Pittswood, turn left up High House Lane. After about 600 yards you will see a path on the right that strikes slightly downhill towards the distant Hadlow College. Follow this path until it joins a track and then walk down the track through the college grounds to return to the tearooms.

The tearooms are open Monday to Saturday from 9 to 5 and from 10 to 4 on Sundays. They serve some cracking cakes and baguettes with light lunches available from noon to 2pm.

Walk No. 9   Appledore

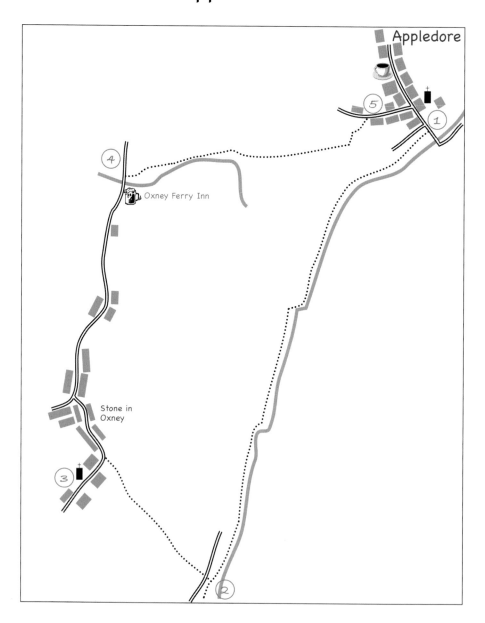

9 Appledore

Teashop:	Miss Mollett's High Class Tea Room, 26, The Street, Appledore, Ashford, Kent TN26 2BX Tel: 01233 758555
Distance:	4.6 miles
Map:	OS Explorer 125
Parking:	There is plenty of parking in The Street
Public Transport:	Appledore is on the rail network, though the station is about half a mile east of the village.
Conditions:	An easy walk over generally level ground and surfaced paths that run alongside the Royal Military Canal for most of its length.

The Walk

1) Head south along The Street, leaving the village down a short hill to reach the bridge over the Royal Military Canal. Turn right on the nearside bank along a footpath signposted as part of the Royal Military Canal Path.

In 1804 Napoleon Bonaparte was Emperor of the French. He had defeated Austria, Prussia and Russia and had reduced the small states of Italy and Germany to obeying his orders. Spain was allied to France and only Britain remained defiant. Napoleon had imposed a trade embargo on Britain and was determined to invade and conquer these islands. The main defence for Britain was, of course, the Royal Navy. But land defences were needed in case the navy failed. The Royal Military Canal was a key element in those defences.

The ports along the south coast were refortified with artillery bastions and specialised strongpoints known as Martello Towers. However, the wide, gently shelving beaches of the Romney Marsh peninsula were thought to be particularly vulnerable to a landing by French troops - and they were too extensive to be guarded along their entire length. The Royal Military Canal was an attempt to cut off the peninsula from the mainland. It

The small tearooms in Appledore are on the high street about 150 yards north of the church.

The World War II pillbox that guards the Royal Military Canal south of Appledore village centre.

was felt that although the beaches could not be held, the shorter line of the canal could. Moreover, the time taken for the French to get ashore would give the defending troops two or three days notice to march reinforcements to the canal defences. The canal was built to skirt the landward side of Romney Marsh, running at the foot of the line of low chalk hills that form the edge of the marsh.

Unlike most canals, the Royal Military Canal was not primarily for the movement of barges. Instead its main purpose was to act as a heavily defended moat. Even in 1804 a water obstacle 60 feet wide and 10 feet deep was a formidable one for any army. To get an army across it complete with supply train and support forces would call for the construction of bridges, which would take several days. The sheer task of fighting across the barrier in the face of determined opposition would take some skill and great numbers, with heavy casualties an unavoidable price to be paid even if the assault were to be successful.

The earth excavated from the canal was piled up on the northern bank to form a key part of the defences. The mound was shaped so that infantry marching along the road behind it could not be seen by observers on the marsh side. Nor could the men be hit by cannonballs fired from the marsh. The top of the mound was shaped to form a firing step, allowing infantry to stand up to shoot at any advancing enemy while protected up to their chest by bullet-proof sods.

At intervals of about 500 yards the canal performed an abrupt dogleg turn before bending back to its original route. In the angle of each dogleg, the mound was shaped into an artillery emplacement. These were designed so that the cannon placed in them could fire along the length of the canal. The idea was that the cannon would mow down any troops attempting to storm over the canal, while at the same time the mound shielded the cannon from any enemy cannon firing from the marsh. No cannon were actually stationed on the canal, it being planned that they would be hauled in by horses when an invasion began.

The complex of the 28-mile-long canal with its attendant earthworks and other structures cost £234,000 and employed 1,500 men to build. It was never used in action as Nelson's great naval victory at the Battle of Trafalgar gave the Royal Navy command of the seas. In 1810 the canal was opened to barge traffic as an attempt by the government to make some money out of the waterway. The canal was never terribly busy as it did not link two major cities, but did remain in use until 1909. The government then sold the eastern section to the town council of Hythe to convert into ornamental waterways and a park, while various landowners bought the rest for use in the complex drainage of Romney Marsh.

In World War II, the government commandeered the canal once again. Pillboxes and concrete gun emplacements were installed in places as the canal was converted into a gigantic tank trap to halt any attempt by German panzers to invade via the marsh. When peace came the canal was returned to civilian use.

The Royal Military Canal Path has now been laid out so that walkers can stroll along all or part of the canal. The canal has become a haven for wildlife. Waterbirds such as swan, heron, kingfisher and moorhen are common here. The margins have become colonised by plants such as yellow flag, water lily and bladderwort. These shelter a multitude of insects,

The Royal Military Canal is now a crucial part of the drainage system for Romney Marsh. The amount of water in the canal can vary dramatically depending on the weather.

including dragonflies, glow-worms and mayfly. The patient observer might glimpse shy mammals such as the watervole or mink.

Almost as soon as you turn on to the Path you will come across one of the artillery bastions, or what remains of it. This example had its ramparts hurriedly flattened in 1940 and the gun platform was used as the base for a pillbox. The pillbox was to be manned in the event of a German invasion - then expected almost any day - with the gun positioned so that it commanded both the bridge over the canal and the B2080 as it ran alongside the canal on its southern bank. As in 1805, the defences of 1940 were thankfully never used.

2) Continue along the path for about a mile and a half. Then turn right along a footpath that crosses the Military Road, now a country lane, before passing over a narrow wooden bridge and then striking off across open fields towards the village of Stone in Oxney. The turning is not signposted - or at least the sign was missing from its post when I did this walk - but don't worry if you miss the turn as the route comes to a surfaced lane about half a mile further on and if you turn right here you will end up in Stone in Oxney. The path skirts a steep hill to the left, then climbs up into the village, meeting a lane at a sharp corner. Turn left to reach the church on your right.

The Church here is an elegant 15th century structure with a fine 62-foot-tall tower. If the tower is open when you call, it is worth the effort of climbing up the stone spiral staircase to reach the top for the magnificent views that it offers over Kent and Sussex. The main point of interest is, however, to be found beside the West Door.

This is a stone altar 2ft long by 1ft 10ins wide and 3ft 4ins high. The top is hollowed out as a basin, and the figure of a bull stands in relief on all four sides. Geological experts say it is made of Kentish ragstone, quarried at Hythe. The altar is generally reckoned to be of Roman workmanship and probably came from the fort at Lympne. The bull carvings have been interpreted in a Christian context as being the symbol of St Luke the Evangelist. However, in a Roman context the bull was more likely to have been a symbol of the pagan god Mithras. It is known that Mithras was a favourite god among the Roman legions, so an altar dedicated to him would be highly likely at a fort. Perhaps this stone altar was originally sacred to Mithras, but was later reused as a Christian object. Either way, it is often said that this ancient stone gave its name to the village.

3) Retrace your steps back along the lane, passing the spot where the path emerged on to the lane, and follow it into the village. At a T-junction turn right.

This village marks the far eastern end of the area known as the Isle of Oxney. This was an island in fact as well as name in Roman times, separated from the mainland by an arm of the sea more than a mile wide. By the 13th century, the island was separated from the mainland by a wide belt of tidal marshland through which flowed the River Rother. In the later 17th century the river changed course to flow south of Oxney, as it still does today on its way to enter the sea at Rye. The marshes became less wet and in the 1750s were the subject of a drainage scheme that turned them into damp pasture land. Today there is little sign that Oxney was ever an island, though you will notice that the land north of the village is low lying and flat.

4) Continue north from the village, dropping down a slight slope to reach what was once the sea floor. After passing the Oxney Ferry Inn you will cross a bridge over a stream known

The sign that marks the spot where the walk strikes out across open fields north of the Oxney Ferry Inn.

as the Reading Sewer. Immediately beyond the bridge take a path on the right that runs across a meadow beside the stream. This is a section of the Saxon Shore Way long-distance footpath.

5) The path will eventually emerge on to a lane named Court Lodge Road. Turn right to return to Appledore and The Street. At the junction with The Street, turn left to find Miss Mollett's High Class Tea Room.

Appledore began life as a port at the mouth of the River Rother. When the river changed its course, the port was left high and dry - literally. As an alternative source of income, the town's elders got permission from Edward II to hold a regular market in The Street. That the market did keep the town reasonably wealthy can be deduced from the fact that a raiding party of Frenchmen who landed in Kent in 1380 during the Hundred Years War made straight for Appledore. Most of the locals got away safely, taking their valuables with them, so the French took their revenge by burning the town to the ground. The church, dedicated to St Peter and St Paul, was rebuilt after the raid and it is this structure which still stands today.

The raid of 1380 seems to have brought an end to Appledore as a prosperous town. Thereafter it acted as a market town for the local area only and gradually slipped into the rural tranquillity that it knows today.

Walk No. 10 Sandwich

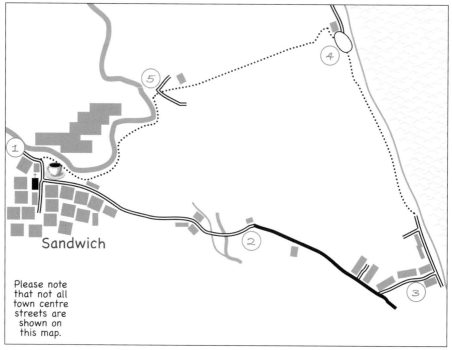

Sandwich

Please note
that not all
town centre
streets are
shown on
this map.

The medieval archway through Fisher Gate that leads from The Quay to the old town centre.

10 Sandwich

Teashop:	The Secret Gardens of Sandwich Tea Room, at The Salutation, Knightrider Street, Sandwich, Kent CT13 9EW Tel: 01304 612730
Distance:	4.6 miles
Map:	OS Explorer 150
Parking:	There are several car parks in Sandwich
Public Transport:	Sandwich is on the rail network.
Conditions:	This walk includes a mile of coast walking and passes a bird reserve.

The Walk

Parking in Sandwich is difficult due to the narrow streets. There are a number of car parks on the edge of town and you can park in the market place if you are lucky enough to find a spot. Having parked your car, make your way to The Quay, which overlooks the River between Bell Lane and Quay Lane. At the eastern end of The Quay the road bends away from the river to become Knightrider Street. The tearoom is on the left through an arch.

There is a huge amount to see in Sandwich, probably the most charming and best preserved medieval town in Kent. The town was once a major port standing at the southern end of the Wantsum Channel, an arm of the sea which cut the Isle of Thanet off from the rest of Kent. During the medieval period the Wantsum gradually silted up until it vanished altogether. Today the town is linked to the sea by the River Stour which meanders across marshes and mud flats for about 5 miles before it empties into the sea at Pegwell Bay. Only yachts and other small craft can get up the river to the town these days.

As an important port, Sandwich became the focus for invaders and internal wars of all types. There was a land battle here between the English and Vikings in 850 and another in 991, naval battles took place in 1009 and 1048 while in

The impressive tower of food that is served as the set Afternoon Tea for one at the tearoom.

The Quay at Sandwich was once a thriving and bustling port, one of the busiest in England. Today the route to the sea has silted up and the port is open only to small craft.

1217 a French invasion captured the town before being fought off with much bloodshed. The defenders were led by the mayor, who was killed in the fighting. The Mayor of Sandwich still wears black on formal occasions as a mark of mourning for his heroic predecessor. The most significant battle fought at Sandwich, however, came in 1460 during the opening stages of the Wars of the Roses.

The Yorkist Earl of Warwick was in Calais, then an English town, with his small army while the Lancastrians under Queen Margaret were in the ascendancy in England. Margaret ordered an army and fleet to gather at Sandwich under Sir Richard Woodville, Baron Rivers, with orders to capture Calais and do away with Warwick. But Warwick struck first. He sailed into Sandwich Harbour on board half a dozen hijacked German merchant ships, stormed ashore and utterly defeated the Lancastrians in a savage street battle fought through the town. Rivers was captured and hauled off to Calais. The victory put fresh heart into the Yorkists and within two years they had defeated their rivals, at least temporarily.

The narrow, twisting streets of Sandwich contain dozens of medieval houses and three magnificent churches - one of which has the largest wooden roof in the county. It is worth taking the time to explore the town and its shops. This walk, however, embraces the reclaimed land to the east of the town that now cuts off the port from the open sea.

1) Leaving the tearoom, turn left along Knightrider Street. About a hundred yards up Knightrider Street from the river turn left into Sandown Road. Continue along Sandown Road.

About 100 yards along Sandown Road you will see to your left the remains of the town walls of Sandwich. There is not much left in the way of walls here, but the ditch and bank are clearly visible. It was here that the French broke in to kill the mayor during their destructive raid.

2) After over a mile, Sandown Road crosses two bridges and then becomes little more than a track. Continue along this track until it passes King's Avenue on the left and then bears left to become Waldershare Avenue.

3) At the far end of Waldershare Avenue you will find yourself at the coast. Turn left along a track and head north along the coast for about a mile with the sea on your right and a golf course on your left. Eventually you will reach a car park.

This stretch of coastline is dominated by sand dunes and shingle beaches. Much of this area is encompassed by the Sandwich Bay Nature Reserve. This 700-acre reserve is the last untouched area of beach and foreshore, complete with a hinterland of dunes and salt marsh, left in Kent. It is jointly owned and managed by the National Trust and the Royal Society for the Protection of Birds. If you are here at the right time of year you should bring your binoculars to sight a wide

The lane that leads from the town centre out to the beach.

variety of waders and waterfowl that gather here. In sunny weather, bring your swimming costumes to enjoy the beach.

The golf club in question is the prestigious Royal St George's, which has hosted the British Open Championship no fewer than 13 times. The Club was founded in 1887 and prides itself on offering a challenging course. The most difficult hole is saved for last: the 460-yard par 4 Hole 18. This requires two long, well-aimed shots to reach the green, which has a hidden trap in the form of 'Duncan's Hollow', a dip in the ground that will snare the unwary.

4) Bear left from the car park along the well-signposted Stour Valley Walk. This path will take you over the drained marshes to the banks of the River Stour.

5) Cross a lane and continue along the Stour Valley Walk to follow the banks of the Stour

back to Sandwich. By keeping to the Stour Valley Walk signs you should emerge back onto The Quay.

The tearoom is open 7 days a week from 10am to 5pm in summer (April to September incl.) and from 10am to 4pm in winter (October to March incl.) It is normally closed for two weeks at Christmastime. This tearoom offers what must be the most sumptuous and luxuriously tasty afternoon teas in Kent.

The Secret Gardens of Sandwich.

Walk No. 11   Tenterden

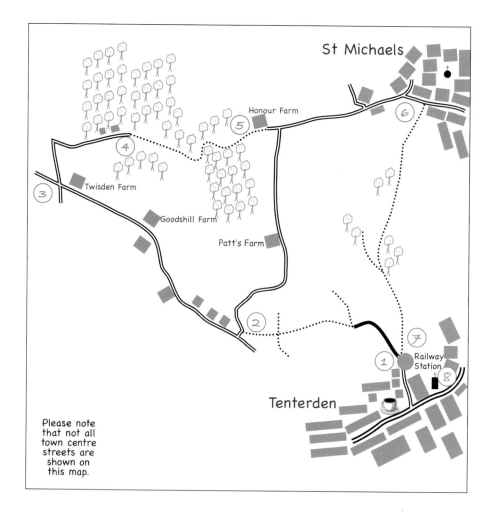

Please note
that not all
town centre
streets are
shown on
this map.

11 Tenterden

Teashop:	Peggoty's Tea Shoppe, 122, High St, Tenterden, Kent TN30 6HT Tel: 01580 764393
Distance:	5 miles
Map:	OS Explorer 125
Parking:	There is parking along the High Street, and in a car park off the High Street.
Public Transport:	Tenterden is on the Stagecoach Bus No.400 from Ashford
Conditions:	This walk is a ramble over the hills north of the town.

The Walk

This walk starts at the railway station because it is both easy to find and has a car park attached. The station is no longer part of the national rail network, but is instead the northern terminus of the Kent and East Sussex Railway. This privately-owned line runs steam trains for families and enthusiasts to Bodiam.

There had been plans for a railway to Tenterden from Ashford or Hastings as early as 1852, but various attempts all fell through either because the military wanted a more southerly route or because of worries that the financial returns would not justify the cost. In 1896, a new law came into effect allowing railways to be built to a lower engineering standard if they were intended for rural areas where light train loads and infrequent services could be expected. This allowed railway companies to build lines more cheaply, making routes to small towns such as Tenterden more likely to be profitable.

The Rother Valley Railway, as the route was known, was approved almost at

The cream tea as served at Peggoty's Tea Shoppe in Tenterden. It also offers a magnificent selection of cakes.

The soaring tower of Tenterden church is dedicated to St Mildred who lived here and died in 720.

once and construction began within weeks. The line opened on 2 April 1900 running from the main line at Robertsbridge through Bodiam and Tenterden to Headcorn.

Although the line was at first a success, it began to lose money in the 1920s and by 1931 was heading for bankruptcy. A drastic reorganisation saw the line converted to using two Ford road busses mounted on metal railway wheels for passengers and cheaper goods wagons. The railway returned to a modest profit and was still struggling along when, along with all other railways in Britain, it was nationalised in 1948. The new British Railways decided it could do without such a minor line turning such small profits and closed it to passengers in 1954. The goods trains continued until 1961, but then they too were discontinued.

Almost at once a group of local railway enthusiasts put forward proposals to run the line as a part-time holiday attraction. The government was unimpressed and laid its own plans to lift the track. Lengthy legal actions followed and after 13 years the Ministry of Transport finally gave way and agreed to sell the line to the charity set up by the enthusiasts. The ministry did, however, impose a condition. The line was to end at Bodiam so that the three level crossings between there and Robertsbridge would not be in use. The line reopened from Tenterden to Wittersham Road in 1973, but the need for expensive repair work to a bridge and other works meant that the full line to Bodiam did not open until 2000.

The line now runs steam trains and other excursions on most weekends of the year and on summer weekdays. There are also special days with various themes. These can vary at relatively short notice, so check the website on www.kesr.org.uk or phone the railway on 01580 762943 if you are intending to ride the trains.

1) *From the railway station head northwest along a track that heads to Pittlesden Manor Farm. Beyond the farm the track bends sharp left and enters woodland. On the far side of the woodland it ends and divides into two footpaths. Take the left-hand path that heads almost directly due west with a patch of woodland on the left.*

2) *This path emerges onto a narrow lane. Here you have a choice. The shorter route follows a peaceful, quiet lane that cuts off about half the walk. If you take the longer route you are faced not only by a steep hill, but also by walking for about half a mile alongside a fairly busy main road, but the walk back through woodland is enchanting. It is up to you. To take the short route turn right and walk along a lane to point 5. To take the longer route, turn left. Almost at once you will reach a T-junction. Turn right along the busy road known as Goods Hill.*

3) *Pass Goodshill Farm on the right, then Twisden Farm. At a crossroads turn right into Millpond Lane and follow this lane round to the right.*

4) *Just past a patch of woodland on the left and a house this narrow lane becomes little more than a footpath.*

5) *Passing Honour Farm on the left Millpond Lane again becomes a lane and then becomes Grange Road. If you took the shorter route you will rejoin the walk here. Continue on past Silcocks Farm on the left.*

6) *At a Y-junction bear right. You are now entering St Michael's, formerly a separate village but now a northern suburb of Tenterden. Just before Orchard Road on the left, turn right on*

to a footpath that heads south across open fields and beside woodland to return to Tenterden Station.

7) Continue south past the station on Station Road to reach the High Street in Tenterden. Turn left to visit the church.

The church of St Mildred is a large structure, especially for a fairly small town. The exuberance of this building is explained by the fact that from about 1380 to 1600 Tenterden was a major centre for the weaving industry and was extremely prosperous. It was usual in the later medieval centuries for a town to show its wealth by building itself a fine church. Tenterden did exactly that by pulling down the small, old church and erecting this magnificent structure.

The St. Mildred to whom this church is dedicated was the daughter of Ermenburga, a princess of the Kent royal family, and of Merewald, the third son of King Penda of Mercia. Mildred died about 720 and there is some written evidence to suggest that there was a church built and dedicated to her in Tenterden as early as 730.

One of the Victorian Vicars of this Church, the Rev. Philip Ward, married Horatia Nelson, the daughter of Admiral Lord Nelson who won the Battle of Trafalgar in 1805. Four of their eight children were born in the Vicarage here and the Rev. Ward is buried in the churchyard although Horatia moved to Pinner after his death and is buried there. The Rev Ward is buried in a vaulted tomb just outside the Lady Chapel window. It would seem that by the mid-1800s the Church had become quite dilapidated and subsequent to the death of the Rev. Ward in 1859 a considerable amount of restoration was completed in the Church.

8) After visiting the church head west along the High Street and go past Station Road to reach Peggoty's on the right.

The footpath through the woodlands that heads south back towards the town from point 6 on the walk.

Peggoty's is open Monday

The view across the valley to Tenterden from the quiet lane that forms the shorter route of this walk.

to Saturday 10 to 5 and on Sundays from 11 to 5. As well as a truly wonderful range of scrumptious home-made cakes it offers some general light lunches and some tasty sandwiches.

Walk No. 12   Headcorn

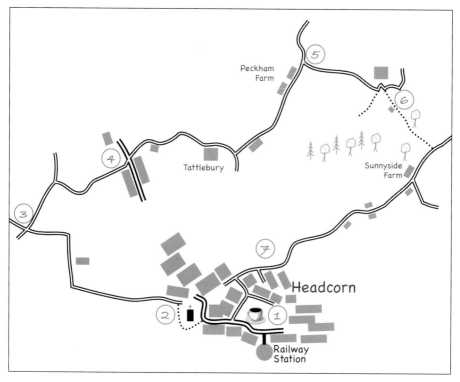

The mangled stump of the famous Headcorn Oak, linked to King John. The decaying stump has been replaced by a new oak grown from an acorn from the original.

12 Headcorn

Teashop:	The Village Tea Rooms, 31-33, High St, Headcorn, Ashford, Kent TN27 9NE Tel: 01622 890682
Distance:	5 miles
Map:	OS Explorer 137
Parking:	There is plenty of parking in the High Street, but at busy times you may need to use the large car park beside the church.
Public Transport:	Headcorn is on the rail network
Conditions:	A route over generally level ground north of the village using surfaced paths or lanes for most of the route.

The Walk

1) From the Village Tea Rooms walk west along the High Street. Where the main road bends sharp right, continue straight on along a narrow lane to the Church.

Headcorn is mentioned in a legal document of 724, by which time it was already a well-established village. It is mentioned again in 785, but then vanishes from the written record until 1222 when a man named Henry of Ospringe was appointed to be the local vicar by no less a personage than King Henry II himself. Quite why the parish merited such royal attention is unclear, but Headcorn was obviously favoured as it was granted the right to a weekly market and annual fair by King Henry III. It was, however, the weaving industry that made Headcorn rich in the 14th century and which enabled the village to tear down its small 11th century church to erect the large structure to be seen today. Excavations have shown that the chancel of the modern church covers the whole of the old church, so the increase in size was massive. The south aisle and tower were added about a century after the main rebuilding.

Near the south door of the church can be found what remains of the Headcorn Oak. According to local tradition, King John sat in the shade of this oak tree to eat a lunch and watch bull-baiting. Given that John reigned from 1199 to 1216, and that the tree must have been a fair size then, this oak must be very old indeed. In 1878 Robert Furley, a great tree expert of his day, took various measurements and concluded that the tree had been planted in about 700 or so. More recent estimates have disputed that the tree is quite that old, but it is undoubtedly ancient. Unfortunately the last signs of life from the ancient trunk came in the summer of 1996 and it is generally now considered to be dead.

2) Having viewed the church and the Headcorn Oak, bear right past the church to emerge onto a lane called Moat Road. Turn left. Follow this lane over a crossroads, round a sharp

A sheep grazes peacefully in a field near Tattlebury.

bend to the right and a second to the left to reach a second crossroads.

3) Turn right at this crossroads, then right again at a Y-junction. This lane emerges on to the A274.

4) Cross the A274 with care and continue straight on along Tattlebury Road to a Y-junction. Turn left.

5) Just beyond Peckham Farm turn right along Boy Court Lane.

6) This lane will turn sharp left, then sharp right then sharp left again. At this second left turn you should continue straight on along a footpath that strikes across open fields, passing a barn, across a small stream and more fields to emerge on to Lenham Road. Turn right.

7) Follow Lenham Road back into Headcorn. Having passed Knights Way on the left, turn left down Forge Lane and follow this street back to the High Street. Turn left to return to the Village Tea Rooms on your left.

The Village Tea Rooms are open seven days a week from 9 to 4, though they will serve tea and buns rather later if you are lucky. In the evenings of Thursday, Friday and Saturday the tearooms become a rather natty little bistro. There is also a gift shop.

If you have the time after tea, walk further east along the High Street, then turn right down the narrow lane that leads to the railway station. It is unfortunate that the original station erected in the 1840s was demolished in the 1980s and the only remains of the old station are the platforms. They do, however, retain a special place in British military history. During the evacuation of the British army from Dunkirk in 1940, the docks at Dover were terribly overcrowded so the main priority was to get the surviving soldiers loaded onto trains and

The arch of trees that covers Boy Court Lane, providing welcome shade in summer and cover from inclement weather in winter.

out of Dover as fast as possible. Headcorn was the first stop for the troop trains. It was here that the men were given their first hot meal on English soil from huge temporary camp kitchens set up on the platforms. The frantic activity lasted for two weeks, then the evacuation was over and the kitchens were packed up and sent away.

The walk leaves Boy Court Lane over this stile. There are several footpaths leaving the lane so be sure to take the correct one.

Walk No. 13 Burmarsh

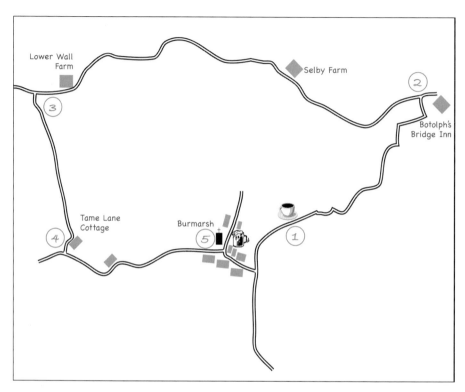

From the lane near Selby Farm the hills to the north are crowned by Lympne. On top of the hill stands the medieval church and castle, while near its foot are the ruins of the Roman fortified port that stood here when Romney Marsh was composed mostly of tidal sands.

13 Burmarsh

Teashop:	**Lathe Barn Tearooms, Donkey St, Burmarsh, Romney Marsh, Kent TN29 0JN Tel: 01303 873618**
Distance:	**7 miles**
Map:	**OS Explorer 138**
Parking:	**The tearooms have their own car park**
Public Transport:	**There are no public transport links to Burmash**
Conditions:	**This walk is long, but easy over surfaced paths and lanes around the drained marshes of Shepway.**

The Walk

1) The Lathe Barn Tearooms have their own car park, so you should start from there. Leaving the car park turn left and head northeast along the narrow, twisting lane.

This entire walk takes you across the flat pasture lands of Romney Marsh. In Roman times there was no land here at all, merely a vast stretch of tidal sandbanks. Over the following years a combination of falling sea levels, silt brought down by local rivers and deliberate land reclamation has resulted in the sandbanks becoming a marsh and finally productive - though very damp - grazing land.

In the early 19th century this area of the marsh was the favoured operating ground of the Bluecoats gang of smugglers based at Aldington a couple of miles to the north. Led by Cephas Quested and George Ransley, the gang avoided the vicious brutality of the notorious Hawkhurst Gang (see the Goudhurst Walk for details) and preferred to use bribery rather than threats to gain the co-operation of local farmers and others. Exactly when the gang began operating is unknown as they seem to have been very good at avoiding the notice of the forces of law and order. They were certainly well established and running a hugely profitable operation when they ran into trouble in 1820.

The appropriate sign that indicates the location of the Lathe Barn tearooms.

A sheep grazes peacefully on Romney Marsh with the hills that made up the medieval coastline visible beyond.

One night that year a patrol of revenue men happened to chance upon the gang as they were unloading a boat of smuggled goods on Camber Sands. A brisk fight broke out. Quested was found lying in a field next morning, both drunk and badly bruised. He did not explain what had happened to him, but was hauled off for trial. He was hanged.

The gang was then led by Ransley on his own, but although he proved to be highly adept at securing good deals with French exporters and had an excellent distribution network across southern England, he lacked Quested's knack of making friends with farmers and fishermen. He also allowed tough, violent outsiders to join the gang and they proved themselves prone to robbery with violence when no shipment was due in. The gang gradually lost the support of local people.

The turning point came in the spring of 1826 when the gang were using a fishing smack to bring contraband in to Dover. A revenue man named Richard Morgan thought that the boat looked suspicious for some reason, called a colleague and set off to search the boat. He had no sooner hailed the boat to stop when a man, probably Ransley's father-in-law, pulled out a gun and shot Morgan dead.

Morgan had been a very popular local man and the brutal killing turned the Dover folk against the Bluecoats. The authorities were soon awash with information about the gang, its members and how it operated. The revenue men sent for reinforcements and in a single day arrested 18 gang members, catching Ransley at home in bed. It is thought that none of the gang escaped. All were transported to Australia for life.

2) Just before reaching Botolph's Bridge Inn, turn left along a lane that cuts back to the west. Follow this lane past Selby Farm and Lower Wall Farm.

3) Just beyond Lower Wall Farm, turn left along a lane.

4) At Tame Lane Cottage turn left again to pass Forty Acre Cottage and reach Burmarsh village itself.

Burmarsh takes its name from the Old English " Burhwaramersc", which means "the fortress in the marsh". There has only been limited archaeological work carried out here, but no trace of a fortress has ever been found. However, in the days before the Norman Conquest, most 'fortresses' were wooden structures that relied more on the armed men they contained than on fortifications for their effectiveness. It is likely that the 'fortress' in question was built during the Viking wars to act as a refuge for the men of the marsh, and perhaps to control any landing spots in the area. The Vikings were adept at moving along a coast in their ships looking for a convenient spot to beach their ships and come ashore to pillage the surrounding area. Having a force of tough armed men on hand would dissuade the smaller raiding parties from trying their luck.

The Church of All Saints, on your left as you enter the village, was built in about 1170 or so on the site of an earlier and smaller church that may have been put up in about 950. The door is Norman in date and has a rather unusual and very grotesque head peering at the visitor from its top. Much of the original doorway has been infilled, presumably to stop cold air coming in during winter services. The church was modernised and restored in the 1870s, sweeping away much of the clutter that had built up over the previous century or so. The chancel arch is thought to be original, but the screen in it is less than a century old as it commemorates two local men killed during the First World War. In the nave is a bell weighing 8 hundredweight which has the inscription NOMEN MAGDALENE CAMPANA GERIT MELODIE. As you will be able to see, it is cracked which is why it is here and not up in the tower with the other six bells.

5) In the village turn right at the T-junction by the Shepherd & Crook Inn, and then left at a second T-junction. This lane will return you to the Lathe Barn.

The lane across the marsh that runs from Lower Wall Farm south to Tame Lane Cottage. This walk is over land that is almost entirely flat.

Lathe Barn offers afternoon teas of home-baked scones and cakes, free-range eggs, local strawberries (when in season) and ice-cold milk shakes. Special children's teas are available for younger visitors. There are also light lunches of crispy salads, jacket potatoes, ploughman's with warm crusty bread and a selection of toasted sandwiches, followed by ice-cream sundaes or delicious homemade puddings.

In the summer (1 April to 30 September), they are open on Tuesday to Friday from noon to 5pm, and noon to 6pm on weekends. They are open on Bank Holiday Mondays as per weekends but are closed on normal Mondays. In the winter they are open only at weekends for lunch and you should book before you go.

The site also has a gift shop, bakery and picture framers if that takes your fancy.

Walk No. 14   Goudhurst

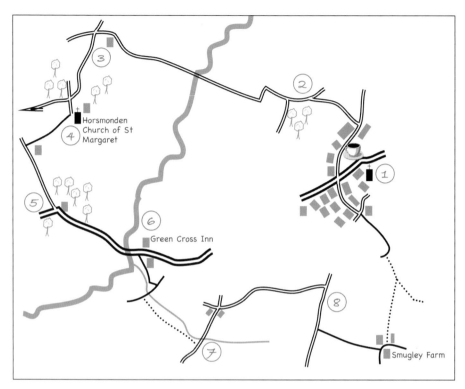

Horsmonden
Church of St
Margaret

Green Cross Inn

Smugley Farm

The churchyard at Goudhurst was the scene of the famous Battle of Goudhurst fought between local farmboys and the infamous Hawkhust Gang in 1747, which left three men dead and dozens injured.

14 Goudhurst

Teashop:	Weeks Bakery & Tea Rooms, 12, High St, Goudhurst, Cranbrook, Kent TN17 1AG Tel: 01580 211380
Distance:	6 miles
Map:	OS Explorer 136
Parking:	There is on-street parking in Goudhurst
Public Transport:	Goudhurst is on Arriva bus route 26 from Marden railway station.
Conditions:	This is a hilly walk that crosses the River Teise twice and takes in part of the route of a dismantled railway.

The Walk

1) Find the church in the centre of the village

This Church of St Mary is a real treasure. The earliest record of a church on this dramatic hilltop site was in 1119, but quite obviously it was not new then and there is some evidence to suggest that the first church here was built some centuries earlier. No doubt this early structure was of wood, and it may have been one of the very first Christian sites in England.

To the practised eye the tower looks slightly squat and out of proportion. This is because when it was built in the 1320s it was at least 20 feet taller and was topped by an elegant spire. Then in 1637, on a hot and sultry summer day a bolt of lightning flashed down from the sky. The spire took the full force of the strike, bursting into flames. When the fire was eventually put out it was found that not only was the spire beyond repair, but that the upper parts of the tower were shattered beyond use. They were taken down and the tower acquired its present height. Despite this blow, the hilltop position ensures that anyone who climbs up the tower - and it is usually open during the day - is rewarded with stunning views across Kent. One enthusiastic local armed with a telescope has claimed to have counted 51 churches in view from the tower. Certainly on a clear day you can see quite clearly both Canary Wharf Tower in central London to the north and the tower of Lympne Church far to the south.

Inside the church is a fine collection of tombs and brasses commemorating members of the two local landowner families: The Bedgeburys and the Culpepers. The 1537 tomb of Sir Alexander Culpeper and his wife boasts two fine and very rare wooden effigies.

The village takes its name from the old Saxon "guth hyrst", which means "fight hill". Whether this commemorates some long forgotten battle or some minor local scuffle that gave its name to the hill is unclear. Certainly no battle here has entered the written record, but given the poorly documented history of early Kent this is hardly surprising.

One fight that certainly did happen here was the savage struggle that heralded the downfall of the Hawkhurst Gang in 1747. The Hawkhurst was the most notoriously violent and vicious gang of criminals active in England in the mid-18th century. Unlike Dick Turpin and other dashing highwaymen, the Hawkhurst Gang was as nasty a piece of work as could be imagined. The gang members were based at the village of Hawkhurst, but made the Mermaid Inn in Rye the base for their smuggling activities. The gang was led by Arthur Gray with Thomas Kingsmill as his second in command.

The gang made a lot of money from smuggling, but also ran extensive protection rackets, wrung extortion from farmers and robbed houses at will. Anyone who objected was beaten to a pulp, had their property burned or both. The villagers on which the gang preyed were cowed into silence by sheer terror. It is known that the gang murdered at least 8 men and killed as many more in shoot-outs with the forces of law and order.

The West Door of Horsmorden Church is rarely opened, but the church itself is usually unlocked and contains some magnificent modern stained glass. The old glass was destroyed when a V1 flying bomb came down here in July 1944.

Then, in 1747, a Goudhurst man named George Sturt came home after many years away with the army, where he had attained the rank of corporal. Sturt was horrified by the situation. He persuaded the men of Goudhurst that they should protect their homes and families. Sturt obtained guns for the men from somewhere and began drilling them in military tactics, accurate firing and bloodthirsty bayonet drill. The Hawkhurst Gang got to hear about the unofficial Goudhurst Militia and sent a chilling message to the village. Unless by 21 April 1747 Sturt had left the village and all weapons had been handed over, then the gang would burn down every house and kill every man in Goudhurst.

On the appointed day some 40 men of the gang marched into Goudhurst. Sturt had his men drawn up in the churchyard. The gangsters charged, but the local farmboys responded with a disciplined volley that cut down George, brother to Thomas Kingsmill. Thereafter the savage fight became a matter of exchanging musket fire for more than half an hour. Then a determined bayonet charge by Sturt and his men sent the gang fleeing. Three Hawkhurst gangsters were left dead and many others had been wounded. The stout villagers of Goudhurst had only cuts and minor wounds.

The view back to Goudhurst from Horsmonden Church. The village occupies the summit of the hill with the church at the highest point.

The Battle of Goudhurst, as the event was soon known, broke the Hawkhurst Gang. Suddenly villagers across Kent were no longer as afraid of the gang as they had been. Within a short time the magistrates had the names of the leaders of the gang. They were given 40 days to surrender for trial or face an automatic death sentence, and a reward of 500 pounds was put up for their capture. Grey and Kingsmill were caught and hanged, several others given long sentences and only one of the named men escaped punishment, by fleeing to France.

Having viewed the church head west along Church Road. You will pass Weeks Tea Rooms on your right. At the crossroads turn right along North Road, the B2079. After about 200 yards turn left down the narrow Blind Lane. This ends in a T-junction.

2) Turn left along Lidwells Lane. Follow this narrow lane as it twists down the hill to cross the River Teise beyond Trottenden Farm.

The Teise was subjected to a huge amount of landscaping and drainage works in the 1950s. This included the removal of mills, the introduction of weirs and the cutting off of many meanders. This led to a drastic change in the meadows, which were drained so that they became drier and less prone to flooding. The inevitable result was that the river became much less attractive to wildlife while heavy rains resulted in water gushing down the straighter, deeper riverbed to cause water levels to rise much quicker in the Medway, into which the Teise empties. The results of some of this work can be seen from the bridge as you cross the river.

3) At a crossroads turn left along a narrow lane that leads to a second crossroads. Turn left to reach Horsmonden Church.

Compared to the violent history of St Mary's, this church of St Margaret has had a very quiet life. It was built in the 1320s by the wealthy vicar, Henry de Grofhurst. His memorial brass still lies in the chancel floor. Also buried here is John Read (1760-1847), a local man and keen gardener who achieved fame by inventing a stomach pump

A selection of the small cakes on offer at the teashop in Goudhurst.

that could empty a person's stomach of suspect food or drink both painlessly and harmlessly.

The only puzzle about the church is why it stands here on a gentle slope above the Teise, not in the village itself a mile to the north. According to local legend, the village used to be clustered around the church, but when the Black Death struck the survivors abandoned the pestilential site and moved north, returning only to worship God.

Archaeologists have confirmed that the medieval village was around the church, but unfortunately for the tale the new village did not form until about 150 years after the Black Death. Perhaps there was something about the little valley where the village now stands that was simply more attractive. There is a spring of pure, sweet water for a start.

4) Just before the traffic island north of the church, turn right on a track and go across the face of the hill to reach a lane. Turn left.

5) The track emerges onto the A262. Turn left and continue along the main road to cross back over the River Teise.

The cheerful baker who stands outside the teashop to advertise the special dishes of the day.

6) Just beyond the river turn right

along a track opposite the Green Cross Inn that runs beside a small tributary of the river and some trees. At a T-junction turn right to cross the stream, then almost immediately left along a footpath that runs on the stream bank for some 200 yards to reach a lane.

7) At the lane turn left, then after about 100 yards turn right along a lane that winds for about 300 yards to meet the B2079.

8) Turn right, then left up a track towards Smugley Farm. At Smugley Farm take the footpath heading north that takes you back to Goudhurst.

Weeks Bakery and Tea Rooms are open Monday, Tuesday, Thursday and Friday from 7 to 4. On Wednesdays they close at 2pm. On Saturdays they are open 8 to 4. They are open on Sundays from May to September only, when they are serving from 11 to 4.30. There is an exceptionally wide variety of cakes on offer here - I counted over 20 when I called! They serve a full fried breakfast until 10am, so if that is your thing you could stop here for breakfast and then do the walk.

Walk No. 15   Birchington

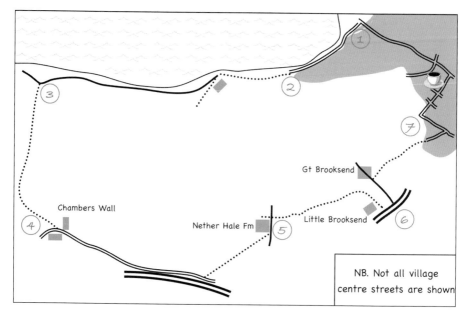

Gt Brooksend

Chambers Wall

Nether Hale Fm

Little Brooksend

NB. Not all village centre streets are shown

The seafront at Birchington is lined by lawns, gardens and benches on which the weary walker may take a rest.

15 Birchington

Teashop:	Victoria's Tea Room, 11, Minnis Rd, Birchington, Kent CT7 9SD Tel: 01843 841800
Distance:	8 miles
Map:	OS Explorer 150
Parking:	There is on-street parking near the tearooms
Public Transport:	Birchington is on the rail network
Conditions:	This walk is mostly over surfaced paths and lanes

The Walk

Victoria's Tea Room is located in a short parade of shops built in the 1930s that retain their original glazed brick frontage.

Victoria's Tea Room stands just 50 yards south of the railway station, which is well signposted, so it is easy to find if you are arriving by train or by car.

The village of Birchington is not in the Domesday Book of 1086, but is first mentioned in 1240.

1) From the tearooms head north past the railway station, over the footbridge that stands to the right of the narrow road bridge and then continue straight on along a fairly uninspired street of 1930s housing. This road will take you to the seafront. Turn left along the seafront, the road is called The Parade. There are some spectacular views here west along the north Kent coast toward the distant towers of Reculver.

2) When the paved road runs out, continue along the paved coastal footpath that forms part of the Wantsum Walk, a formal walk laid out by the council and identified by

The seafront at Birchington where the road runs out and a paved footpath continues along the coast to the distant twin towers of Reculver.

a blue sign featuring a medieval sailing ship. After a couple of hundred yards the path joins a concrete track from the left. Continue straight on along the coast.

This stretch of coastline is protected from the sea by a seawall. You will find a sandy shingle beach to your right and on the left a seemingly endless view of flat farmland. This was formerly the Wantsum itself. In Roman times this was all open sea, though rather shallow. Birchington marked the western shore of what was then a separate island: Thanet. An arm of the sea stretched south from here to Sandwich on the southeastern coast of Kent. What are now the towns of Margate, Ramsgate and Broadstairs were then small villages isolated on the island.

The Romans built two mighty fortified ports to dominate the Wantsum Channel. The northern one was Reculver, where medieval monks later recycled the bricks and stones of the fortress walls to build the two towers you see today as part of their monastery. The southern fortress was at Richborough, just north of Sandwich. The Wantsum remained open to shipping until around the 13th century, providing a convenient sheltered seaway that cut off the exposed run around Thanet. Then a combination of silting and land reclamation closed off the northern end of the Channel, where you are now. By around 1600 the Channel had been reduced to a stretch of open marshes, lakes and streams. Thanet was no longer an island.

Today the marsh has been mostly reclaimed, but in places open water is still to be found. This land remains too wet for arable farming, so most of it is given over to grazing land.

3) Where the track veers left inland slightly there is a Y-junction. Take the left hand path that heads inland with a broad water-filled drainage cut on your right. Cross over the railway line. After a further 400 yards follow the path as it bears left. This path emerges on to a narrow lane at a group of buildings called Chambers Wall.

4) Turn left at Chambers Wall along the lane. The lane will run alongside the very busy A299 for a while, passing a small industrial estate on the left. About 200 yards beyond the industrial estate, turn left off the lane to follow a footpath that strikes out across the grasslands. This section can be damp and sticky after rain.

5) The path emerges onto a track just south of Nether Hale Farm. Turn left up the track, then right along a bridleway heading toward Upper Hale and Brooksend.

6) The bridleway emerges onto the A28 at Little Brooksend Farm. Turn left and walk alongside the main road for about 50 yards to get over a stream. Almost immediately after the bridge, turn left up the track to Great Brooksend Farm. Just before the farm buildings, turn right onto a footpath that goes across the wide open farmland. This path reaches the outer edge of Birchington at Mill Row.

7) Continue straight along Mill Row to the junction with Essex Gardens. Turn left up Essex Gardens. This road bends right into Devon Gardens. This road continues straight on over a junction to become Prospect Road. Continue straight on along Prospect Road to the junction with Station Road. Turn left and you will find yourself back at Victoria's Tea Room. It also specialises in ice creams and is open Tuesdays to Sundays from 9am - 3pm.

Just one of many drainage channels that runs across the flat lowlands across which this walk wanders.

If you are of an artistic frame of mind, you might care to take a slight diversion. Instead of turning left on Station Road, turn right and continue for about 300 yards to find the Church of All Saints, Birchington. This is a rather charming little 14th century building with later additions, but the main point of interest is the tomb of the great Pre-Raphaelite artist Dante Gabriel Rossetti. Although he is best known today as a painter, Rossetti himself reckoned he was a better poet while he became known for his collection of pet wombats. He did not live in Kent, but was visiting a friend in Birchington when he was taken ill and died suddenly at the age of 54.